Working with

OLDER

people

Diane Church

W
FRANKLIN WATTS
LONDON • SYDNEY

Many of the photographs in this book
feature real people in difficult circumstances.
Because of this, some of the photographs may not
be as clear or bright as we would normally wish.

© 2001 Franklin Watts

First published in Great Britain by
Franklin Watts
96 Leonard Street
London EC2A 4XD

Franklin Watts Australia
56 O'Riordan Street
Alexandria
NSW 2015

ISBN: 0 7496 4067 7
Dewey Decimal Classification 362.6
A CIP catalogue record for this book is available from the British Library

Printed in Malaysia

Editor: Kate Banham
Designer: Kirstie Billingham
Art Direction: Jason Anscomb

Acknowledgements
The publishers would like to thank the following people and organisations
for their permission to reproduce photographs in this book:
Abbeyfield: 7; Age Concern: 14, 16 (Neil Walker), 17b (Phillip Polglaze), 26 (Nick Hayes); Alzheimers Disease Society: 24;
Arthritis Care: 10 (Tom Lindsey), 27t; John Birdsall (www.JohnBirdsall.co.uk): front cover, 4, 5b, 21, 23, 25;
British Heart Foundation: 22; Contact the Elderly: 17t; Diane Church: 5t; Elderly Accommodation Council: 19;
Guide Dogs for the Blind Association: 15 (Jon Walter), 27b; Help the Aged: 9, 18; Auriel James: 8; Macmillan Cancer Relief: 20;
RNIB: 13 (reproduced by permission of RNIB © 1998); RNID: 12; Rukba: 6; Science Photo Library: 11 both (Hattie Young).

# Contents

Words printed in **bold** are explained in the glossary.

♥ Getting older

It is hard to imagine that you will ever be as old as your parents and other grown-ups, isn't it? It is even harder to imagine that one day you will be 70 or 80 years old.

One hundred years ago, most people in the UK lived to about the age of 40. Now most people live to about 80 – or even older.

Do you have any friends or relations who are 70 or older?

Older people have much to share with us. They have lived through good and bad experiences and seen many changes in the world.

Today, older people have more fun, go to more places and do more things than they were able to do in the past.

As we get older, we may need some extra help. Many older people cannot see or hear as well as they could when they were younger. They may find they do not have enough money to live on, or that they have no friends or family nearby to help them.

This book explains the many ways charities help older people and why this help is needed.

♥ Somewhere to live

We all need our own space where we can relax and feel at home. Most grown-ups have their own homes, but some older people have to leave their homes because they need extra care or they don't have enough money.

Charity workers often visit older people in their own homes to make sure they are all right.

When older people **retire**, they may not have enough money to stay in their own homes. The Royal United Kingdom Beneficent Association (Rukba) gives some people extra money each week to pay for things like electricity and water, so they are not forced to move house.

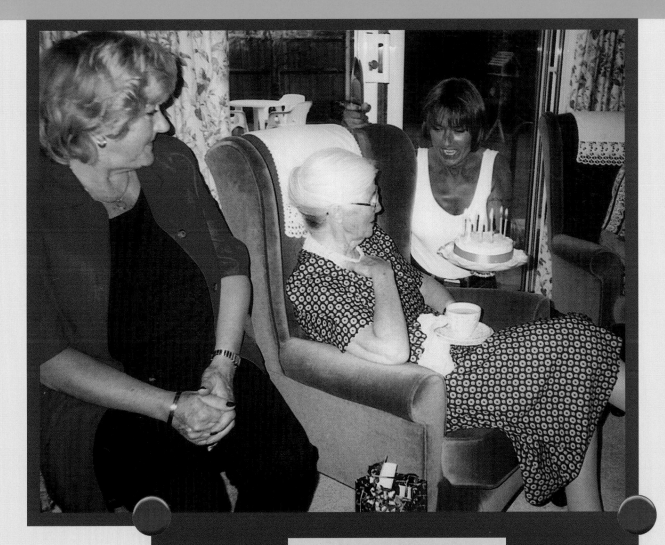

CASE STUDY

Last year Elizabeth was finding it very difficult to look after herself, so she moved into **sheltered accommodation** provided by Abbeyfield. Since moving, Elizabeth has made lots of new friends and is close to local shops. She knows there is always someone nearby if she needs help. 'How glad I am that I came to live here,' says Elizabeth.

♥ Money worries

Sometimes older people do not have enough money to live on. They cannot afford to eat healthy food, heat their homes and buy all the things they need, like clothes.

Auriel James' organisation, Charity Search, helps older people and their families by putting them in touch with various charities.

When Auriel James retired at 65, she was alarmed to find how many older people needed help. So she set up Charity Search. That was more than ten years ago. The charity now gets 5,000 calls a year from older people and their families.

SeniorLine is a service run by Help the Aged. It helps older people, especially those who are frail, lonely or poor, find out how they can get more money to live on.

If you had only a small amount of money to live on, what would you need to buy? What could you do without? Why?

Calls to SeniorLine are free.

♥ Moving around

As you grow up, your body will change.
As you grow older, it will change even more.

When we get old, it can take longer
to recover from illnesses or accidents.
Older people are also more likely to
develop conditions that make it harder
for them to move around.

CASE STUDY

Amy has **arthritis** - a condition that makes it very painful for her to move. Arthritis Care arranges transport so that she can go out and meet her friends, 'It's good to have fun and forget our aches and pains for a while,' says 82-year-old Amy.

A **stroke** is a kind of illness that happens if blood is prevented from reaching part of the brain. After a stroke, it may be hard for a person to move or speak. **Therapists** help people learn to use their bodies again. The Stroke Association helps people by giving them information and advice about their stroke.

This man is using a special breadboard with spikes. The spikes hold the toast steady while he butters it.

A speech therapist is helping this woman learn to talk again after a stroke.

♡ Seeing and hearing

Talking to your friends on the phone and being able to read books or magazines are things that we all take for granted. But some older people cannot see or hear very well, and are unable to do these things. This can make older people feel very lonely and bored.

What other things would you find it hard to do if you couldn't see or hear very well?

The Royal National Institute for the Deaf (RNID) provides text phones so older people can read on a screen what is being said to them.

Now that Doris can no longer see well enough to read, she enjoys listening to Talking Books.

When 77-year-old Doris found she could not see to read, she was very sad. Now she has Talking Books, which are tapes of popular books and stories. They are made by the Royal National Institute for the Blind (RNIB). 'When the Talking Book goes on, I don't feel so lonely,' says Doris. 'It's like having a friend in my sitting room.'

♥ Out and about

It can be difficult for some older people to go out on their own. They may not be able to climb stairs, get on buses or carry heavy shopping.

Age Concern runs minibuses for older people so that they can get out of the house, do the shopping, see their friends and go to the doctors.

← The Age Concern minibuses have special ramps that lift up and down. Then the passengers can get on and off the bus easily.

Seven years ago, 89-year-old Hilda suddenly went blind. The Guide Dogs for the Blind Association provided her with a guide dog to help her.

'Before I had a guide dog I would get lost walking down the street. People thought I was stupid because I was always bumping into things,' explains Hilda. 'Having a guide dog has given me back my dignity.'

Hilda is the oldest person to receive a guide dog from the Guide Dogs for the Blind Association.

How would you get to school if you were blind and had no one to take you?

♥ Making friends

In the past, people were often cared for by their families as they grew older. Nowadays people move around much more and grandparents often live a long way from their children and grandchildren.

How close do you live
to your grandparents?
How often do you
see them?

To stop older people feeling lonely, Contact the Elderly arranges tea parties once a month at different people's houses. Nina is over 90 and she loves going along and talking to Eliot and his twin brother Paul.

Eliot (left) and Paul love it when their mum and dad hold a tea party. They like to hear Nina's stories about long ago.

Age Concern runs day centres across the UK where older people can make friends, have a warm meal and enjoy themselves.

♥ Having fun

When people stop work, they are likely to have many years of enjoyment ahead of them before they need help and care. This is because older people are healthier and are living longer than ever before.

For many people, retirement is the chance to take up new hobbies, travel to new places and make new friends.

Learning a new skill, such as juggling, can help to keep you active.

Older people can join The Dark Horse Venture and learn new skills like story and poetry writing, enjoy sports like rambling and cycling, and help to teach computer skills to children.

It's never too late
to take up
a new hobby.

Nola (82), pictured above, won first prize in an art competition for older people. It was set up by the Elderly Accommodation Council. Nola has had a stroke and cannot move one side of her body, which made her very sad until she started painting. 'Art has given me a new lease of life,' says Nola.

What new hobbies
would you like to try?

♡ Extra help

If you left something in another room, you could probably get it yourself. If you needed to go to the toilet, you could manage on your own.

Older people who are not well or are unable to move often need help.
They may be cared for by their families or someone else may look after them.

Most people prefer to be with their families when they are very ill. Macmillan nurses care for people with **cancer** in their own homes or in hospitals.

Macmillan nurses tell patients and their families all about the treatment they need.

Some older people may need help all the time. This can be very hard work for their carers.

Looking after someone who is elderly and needs lots of care can be very tiring. It is also difficult to get out of the house to go shopping or see friends. Carers UK runs a helpline that listens to carers' problems and helps them feel less stressed.

♥ Preventing problems

There are certain things we all need to do to stay healthy and get the most out of life, like taking regular exercise.

Can you think of any other things we should do to stay healthy?

More people die of heart disease than any other condition in the UK. To get into healthy habits at an early age, the British Heart Foundation tells children how to look after themselves. This should prevent heart disease later in life.

These children are collecting money for research into heart disease, and learning about healthy living at the same time.

Many illnesses and conditions have no cure. We do not know enough about why they develop in the first place.

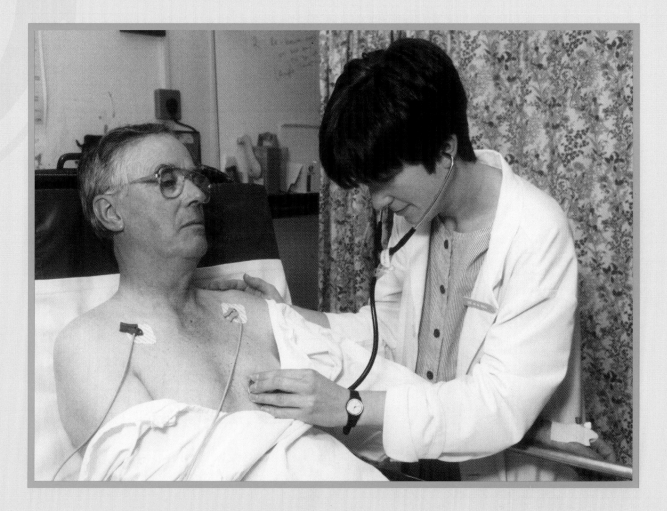

Many charities support research to find answers. It may be that some of the illnesses and diseases people suffer from today will have a cure when you are older.

♥ Young and old

Older people have lived longer, done more things and know more about life than younger people. So older people have a lot to share with you.

Joan, who is in her 70s, was put in touch with Hannah and her family by Age Concern. Hannah's family were having problems and Hannah found it very upsetting. Joan visits Hannah once a week and has become a valuable friend.

← Older people and children can often become good friends.

Children often live a long way from their grandparents so they can't share ordinary things like a shopping trip.

Children today often miss out, as they do not mix much with older people and so do not know what life was like for their families and friends in the past. The Dark Horse Venture is giving older people the chance to record their memories, so that future generations will be able to share their past and wisdom.

Have you ever spoken to an older person about their childhood? How was it different from yours?

♥ Raising money

Charities are able to help others because they are given money to do so. This money is given by people like you and me, raising millions of pounds each year.

The easiest way to help charities is to put money in a collection box. But there are many more fun ways. It doesn't matter how silly or simple the idea is – as long as it helps. You could have a sponsored bike ride or a sponsored silence at your school.

Arthritis Care recently held a pot-painting competition to raise money.

Some charities organise fairs as a way of raising money. There are usually lots of stalls offering different things to do.

How would you raise money to help older people?

This girl is having her face painted to look like her dog.

♥ How you can help

Have you ever helped anyone? It can feel good to do something kind and generous. You can help by:

● contacting a charity that you are interested in (see pages 30 and 31) to find out more about what they do. Many charities have children's clubs that include competitions and games, as well as providing information.

● asking your teacher to get someone from a charity supporting older people to come and talk to your class.

● treating older people you meet with respect.

● getting help from older people in your community for history projects or stories.

● raising some money for the charity of your choice on your own or through your school. Get your parent, carer or teacher to contact the charity to find out more.

Glossary

arthritis — the name given to different conditions that make the body's joints (hips, knees, wrist etc) swollen and very painful.

cancer — when the body produces too many cells which stop nearby parts of the body working properly. Some cancers can be cured, others cannot.

retirement — when someone stops work permanently because they have reached a certain age. In the UK this is usually at 65 years old.

sheltered housing — flats or rented rooms where older people can live knowing that, close by, people are employed to help them at any time.

stroke — when the brain does not get oxygen for a while. As a result, people who have a stroke may not be able to speak properly or use a part of their body. If someone has a severe stroke they may die.

text phone — a machine that shows a caller's words written on a screen, rather than being heard in the receiver.

therapist — someone who treats an illness or condition. A physiotherapist helps people use their bodies properly, and a speech therapist helps people who have difficulty speaking.

♥ Contact details

All the charities in this book do many more things to help older people than those described. Contact them to find out more.

Abbeyfield Society
01727 857536
www.abbeyfield.com
post@abbeyfield.com

Age Concern
020 8765 7200
www.ageconcern.org.uk
ace@ace.org.uk

Alzheimers Disease Society
020 7306 0606
www.alzheimers.org.uk

Arthritis Care
020 7380 6500
www.arthritiscare.org.uk

British Heart Foundation
020 7935 0185
www.bhf.org.uk
artiebeat@bhf.org.uk
(Children's club)

Charity Search
0117 982 2846

Contact the Elderly
020 7240 0630
www.contact-the-elderly.org
HQ@Contact-elderly.demon.
co.uk

The Dark Horse Venture
0151 729 0092
www.darkhorse.rapid.co.uk
darkhorse@rapid.co.uk

Elderly Accommodation Council
020 8789 6185

Guide Dogs for the Blind Association
0870 600 2323
www.guidedogs.org.uk
guidedogs@gdba.org.uk

Help the Aged
020 7278 1114
www.helptheaged.org.uk
info@helptheaged.org.uk
SeniorLine: 0808 800 6565

Macmillan Cancer Relief
020 7840 7840
information line 0845 601 6161
www.macmillan.org.uk
information_line@macmillan.org.uk

Royal National Institute for the Blind
020 7388 1266
Helpline 0845 766 9999
www.rnib.org.uk

Royal National Institute for the Deaf
020 7296 8000
Textphone: 020 7296 8001
www.rnid.org.uk

Royal United Kingdom Beneficent Association
020 7605 4200
charity@rukba.org.uk

The Stroke Association
020 7566 0300
www.stroke.org.uk

Organisations in Australia and New Zealand

Database of Australian Charities
www.auscharity.org.au

Foundation for Aged Care
(02) 9634 0513
www.arv.org.au

Blue Nursing Service
(07) 3377 3333
www.bluecare.org.au

Aged Concern
64-9-6230184

Index